MW01167322

The Apocrypha: Does It Matter?

The Apocrypha: Does It Matter?

A Protestant's View

S. Laws

Copyright © 2012 by S. Laws.
Cover Art by Angie Laws

ISBN: Hardcover   978-1-4691-5049-9
               Softcover   978-1-4691-5048-2
               Ebook   978-1-4691-5050-5

All rights reserved. No part of this book may be reproduced or transmitted in
any form or by any means, electronic or mechanical, including photocopying,
recording, or by any information storage and retrieval system, without permission
in writing from the copyright owner.

This book was printed in the United States of America.

Rev. date: 09/17/2013

To order additional copies of this book, contact:
Xlibris LLC
1-888-795-4274
www.Xlibris.com
Orders@Xlibris.com
94160

CONTENTS

In Dedication

to

Dan, Angela, Danielle, Bryce,
and future generations.

"KEEP THE FAITH"

Introduction

Included within the contents of the Apocrypha, are a group of books that are most commonly excluded in today's Bible. The rules of Judaism and Christianity differ in defining the "Inspired Word" that is honored in their religious readings and their acceptance of these books. Some readers may be wondering what does the definition of the term "Inspired Word" mean. In all honesty, it can mean a lot of things. It may refer to the Koran, John Smith's Book of Mormon or other religious writings. However, I am focusing on the Protestant's Bible containing 66 books. This particular book known as the Bible and generally referred to as the "Inspired Word" uncommonly includes the Apocrypha today.

Among Judaism, the exclusion of the books in the Apocrypha began in the 4th century when Jewish Rabbis refused to adopt it into their Old Testament (also known as the Canon) because it did not meet certain criteria.

The Rabbis' criterion for accepting books into the Canon is based on the three following requirements. First, the Jewish criteria demanded that all books included in the Canon be written in the Hebrew language. Secondly, the writings must contain prophecy. Thirdly, they considered their last prophet to be Malachi who lived before 400 B.C. and excluded all writings after his death. Therefore, the books of the Apocrypha did not make it into the Jewish Canon (Old Testament) because they did not contain prophecy, were not solely written in Hebrew, and were created after the days of Malachi. However, St. Jerome did include them in the Vulgate.

Among Christians, the inclusion began when St. Jerome of the Roman Catholic Church included the Apocrypha books into what became known as the Vulgate. The Vulgate can be termed as the Latin version of today's Bible.

St. Jerome did not adopt the Rabbis' criterion because Christianity became a new era with new ideas through Jesus Christ. A Christian's acceptance of the New Testament (to address the message of Jesus) automatically contradicts the Jewish rules for two reasons. First, the Jewish language rule contradicts the acceptance of the Protestant's New Testament which was written in Greek. Secondly, the last prophet rule contradicts the Christian's recognition of Jesus as prophet and a multitude of prophets that followed him. Therefore, today's Christians cannot embrace the Jewish theory in developing their book of "inspired Word." So why is the Apocrypha missing in most Protestant Bibles today?

It all started with Wycliffe. Wycliffe was the reformer who translated the Bible into the English replacing the common Latin version. In doing this, he also included all books termed Apocrypha with the exception of 4 Ezra. His acceptance was later challenged and rejected in the 17th century by all churches except the Church of England.

As you examine the books of the Roman Catholic Apocrypha, you will find many of the writings provide better clarity and understanding of Jewish culture, social change, and literary writing style during the period before, during, and after the earthly life of Christ. It also provides a transition of religious priorities and sets the stage for the teachings of Jesus Christ.

You will find I have lightly summarized each book. I have summarized them enough to pull out my main objective which is to introduce the common thread found within each one and encourage further Biblical study among truth seekers. All quoted scriptures in this book are obtained from the *Harper Collins Study Bible New Revised Standard Version* unless otherwise noted.

THE APOCRYPHA

ACCORDING TO

ROMAN CATHOLIC

OLD

TESTAMENT

CANON

Dedicated to those

✝

who search for truth.

The Apocrypha's Historical Time-Line

What do we know about the history of the Apocrypha? The historical timeline of the inclusion of the Apocrypha within the Christian Bible reveals a long history of being removed and accepted for various reasons in whole or in parts. An outline of the history of the rejection and acceptance follows in order to understand the many years of confusion and mystery encompassing its questionable validity.

382 A.D

Jerome, composed his Latin version (the Vulgate) using the preferred Hebrew. At first, he only included Esther and Daniel. Later, upon the suggestion of two bishops, he added Tobit and Judith. However, he did not support their additions as important in establishing and supporting doctrinal beliefs.

1382 A.D.

Over one thousand years passed by since the death of Christ. A man named Wycliffe translates the Bible from the Vulgate and includes all of the Apocrypha with the exception of 4 Ezra.

1534 A.D.

One Hundred and fifty-two years later, Martin Luther, the great reformist who broke away from the Catholic church and formed the Protestant religion was influenced by Jerome's writing (see 382 A.D.) and the opinion of other authorities. He placed the books of the Apocrypha at the end of the Old Testament in his 1534 publication. Although he believed these books should be included in the Bible, he did not consider them enlightening or holy.

1546 A.D.

Twelve years later, The Council of Trent (A religious group existing within the Catholic church between 1545 and 1563 to address the issues of the Protestant reformation) supported the authenticity of the Apocrypha by adding it back into the Roman Catholic Bible. All books were added with the exception of 1-2 Esdras and the Prayer of Manasseh. However, although these writings were not added into the Bible, they can be found in the 1592 Vulgate. This was confirmed by the First Vatican council in 1870.

1599 A.D.

Fifty-three years later, the Apocrypha was removed from the Geneva Bible. During the 17th century, some believed this was a mistake because the volumes appeared in the Table of Contents in Calvinism's Westminster Confession (1646-1648).

17th Century

All printings of the KJV Bible (except for the Church of England's) did not include the Apocrypha.

1827

The British and Foreign Bible Society did not support "sister organizations" in Europe that produced Bibles containing the Apocrypha. Shortly afterwards, the American Bible Society started printing Bibles without the Apocrypha too. This reduced the size of the Bible and its contents which also lowered the costs of production and reduced the purchase price for consumers.

Mid-20th Century

By the mid-20th Century, (After the Qumran Cave findings) many scholars began to recognize the valuable information contained in the books. Scholars found that the information in the Apocrypha gives its readers a better understanding of Jewish history prior to its Christian origins. Translations such as the Revised Standard Version (RSV), New Revised Standard Version (NRSV), and Today's English Version (TEV) are commonly known to include the Apocrypha.

The timeline information was obtained from Eerdman's Dictionary[1] and gives us general information to help us understand why the Apocrypha is not commonly taught in most churches today.

In summary, the Apocrypha was never used to establish or support doctrine; however, it is and was agreed by many to contain valuable information.

---

[1] *Eerdmans Dictionary of the Bible*. Wm B. Eerdmans Publishing Co. Grand Rapids, MI 49503. 2000

Book of
Tobit

Introduction

A book found in the Apocrypha according to Roman Catholic, Greek, and Slavonic Bibles is Tobit. It is a fiction story about a very religious Israelite, his wife and children. It was probably written between the third and fourth century B.C.E.

This story embraces Jewish culture and rituals practiced by the Jews during this period. The main character, Tobit, is a pious Jew that strictly follows Jewish laws and rituals. The story centers around Tobit's life, his family, and friends and entertains its reader with a variety of life situations such as marriage, traditions, foods, family, angels, religion, and duties to the poor.

The writer also describes how God's people are not always blessed, but sometimes endure difficult times because of the sinfulness of the "demonic realm" as described in the NRSV Harper Collins Study Bible[2]. In order for Tobit to make sense of the difficulties he encounters, he comes to the conclusion that everything will end happily as long as he is focused on the final outcome just as Job (a character from an Old Testament book titled "Job") did.

According to some theologians, the terminology in this book contradicts itself in some ways. One particular concern among theologians is found in Chapter 1 verse 9. In this text, it states that Tobit married a member of his family. Since the practice of inter-marriage is banned

---

[2]   *The Harper Collins Study Bible: New Revised Standard Version.* Society of Biblical Literature. Harper San Francisco. Fulham Palace Road, London W6 8JB. 1989 (pg 1437)

under Jewish law, it is difficult to believe he actually married his blood sister. It is very possible that the translation has lost its meaning and the word "family" is in reference to tribe, not family as Americans define it today. Anyone who has ever studied Greek and/or Hebrew realizes how the original interpretation can be difficult to translate into other languages. Interesting enough, this same problem of translation is also mentioned later by Sirach's grandson in the prologue of Ecclesiaticus, or the Wisdom of Jesus Son of Sirach which is also included in the Apocrypha and written around that same time period.

Summary

The book of Tobit is a story that details many ideas, concepts, and cultures that can also be found within the books of the Minor Prophets, Torah, and New Testament. In the first chapter, the writer describes how the fictitious character named Tobit religiously followed the ways of "truth and righteousness." Tobit also provides to the needy among his people before his exile to Nineveh. Although his people offer sacrifices to King Jeroboam's calf, Tobit does not follow the crowd. He continues to worship the one and only God of Israel. He abstains from eating the foods of the Gentiles because he loves God with all his heart and eats only those things commanded by laws of the Torah.

In the beginning of the story, Tobit is in good standing with a ruler named Shalmaneser and he was able to purchase all the things he needed. During that time he provided to the poor of his tribe, and buried the dead who were tossed over the wall of Nineveh. However, after Shalmaneser's death, the roads became unsafe upon the reign of Shalmaneser's son, and the change of leadership prevented Tobit from making trips on the roadways to purchase kosher foods.

Tobit was known to secretly bury the Israelites that were killed by King Sennacherib as he fled from Judea in the days of judgment, and his burial of the victims troubled King Sennacherib. You see, during that period, decomposing dead bodies were looked upon as decorations symbolizing the victory of the executor. I must admit, I find this to be a gruesome display of power, however; this was the king's ritual during this period. King Sennacherib was not pleased to find the bodies missing when he returned to the areas of his murders. One day, a Ninevite told the king about Tobit's secrete burial tactics, and word quickly spreads that the King is in search of Tobit with plans to kill him. Upon hearing this news, Tobit becomes fearful and runs off. All of his property is seized and retained by the royal treasury. The only thing left behind is his wife, Anna, and his son, Tobias.

No more than forty days after Tobit's property is seized and he leaves town, two sons of Sennacherib murder King Sennacherib and take flight to the mountains of Ararat. Esar-haddon, a son of Sennacherib, reigns afterwards. The new king selects a man named Ahikar (who is also the nephew of Tobit) to serve in a leadership position over the accounts of his kingdom and administration. Ahikar intercedes for Tobit's return, and Tobit is allowed to came back to Nineveh.

Chapter 2: This chapter, although fiction, brings out and ties together a festival that merges the Old and New Testament together. At the beginning of the second chapter in verse 1 the main character, Tobit, describes a great dinner that was prepared for him during the festival of weeks which he also describes as the festival of Pentecost:

> "At our festival of Pentecost which is the sacred festival of weeks . . . "

Before Tobit sits down to a fine dinner prepared for him, he asks his son to find all the poor and bring them back to eat with them. While his son is out gathering the poor, his son finds one of their own people dead. This person had been killed and tossed into the market place. His son tells his father who immediately gets up from the table before eating to get the body from the market place. He returns, washes up, and recalls a scripture stating their festivals will become a time of mourning and their songs lamentations. He begins to sob.

After the sun goes down, Tobit goes to dig a grave and buries the man. His neighbors laugh at him because he continues to bury the dead although he has fearfully suffered much for doing this in the past. That evening, Tobit washes up and goes to the courtyard to sleep. Because it is so warm, he sleeps with his face uncovered. His eyes become covered by bird droppings left by the sparrows sitting on the wall above him. The more the doctors treat him for this condition, the worse his eyes become until he is completely blind for four years. Tobit's nephew, Ahikar, takes care of him for two years before leaving to Elymais.

Tobit and a young lady named Sarah, pray to God about their on-going tribulations. They are both distressed and pray for death. Sarah has been married seven times, and immediately after each marriage, her husband is killed by the mythical demon named Asmodeus. She too is laughed at within her community. Her father's maid wishes Sarah dead in chapter 3 verse 9 and hopes Sarah never conceives a son or daughter.

God hears the prayers of Tobit and Sarah and prepares to answer them. In the meantime, Tobit prepares for death and gives burial instructions to his son Tobias in chapter 4. He tells Tobias that although they are currently poor, he left a treasure with Gabael son of Gabrias at Rages in Media and sends Tobias to collect it. Tobit instructs Tobias to maintain the wealth and flee from all sin.

Angels in Unawares

In chapter 5, Tobias listens to his fathers instructions and chooses a traveling companion who is actually an angel named Raphael. Tobias does not realize he has chosen an angel (verse 4). He was an angel in unawares as referred to in the New Testament in Hebrews 13:2:

> "Do not neglect to show hospitality to strangers, for by doing that some have entertained angels without knowing it." (NRSV)

Tobit meets the guide, Raphael, and explains to him that he is blind and near death. Raphael explains to Tobit that he will be healed. Tobit insists that Raphael share his name and kinsman with him. Confusion occurs within the story when the angel Raphael introduces himself to Tobit as Azariah (verse 13) without any explanation. (Readers need to remember this as you continue through the story.) After Tobias leaves with the angel and dog, Sarah tells Tobit she is unhappy about his decision to send their only son off on a journey. Tobias consoles her and addresses his wife as sister in Chapter 5 verse 21. (I believe the word "sister" refers to tribal association—not blood relative.)

In chapter 6, during the trip, Tobias is washing his feet at the Tigris river when a fish jumps out of the water and grabs a hold of his foot. He cries out and the angel tells him to grab hold of the fish. Tobias did, and the angel told him to slice it open and remove its gall, heart, liver, and throw away the intestines. The angel, Azariah (aka Raphael), informs Tobias that these organs could be used as medicine in the following scripture:

> " . . . As for the fish's heart and liver, you must burn them to
> make a smoke in the presence of a man or woman afflicted
> by a demon or evil spirit, and every affliction will flee away
> and never remain with that person any longer. And as for the
> gall, anoint a person's eyes where white films have appeared
> on them; blow upon them, upon the white films, and the eyes
> will be healed." (chapter 6: 8-9 NRSV)

As the story goes on, Raphael tells Tobias he will marry Sarah, and Raguel approves the marriage of Tobias to his daughter because they are kinsman (**of the same tribe**) upon their marriage to each other. Raguel says:

" . . . Take your kinswomen; from **now on** you are her brother
and she is your sister." (Chapter 7:11 NRSV)

I have placed the words in bold that shows a relationship change
between Tobias and Sarah that begins with their marriage and makes
them "brother and sister." This reference is like a brotherhood. It can be
found in the New Testament as well. Jesus said:

" . . . My mother and my brothers are those who hear the word
of God and do it." (Luke 8:21 NRSV)

Tobias and Sarah become married. On their wedding night, Tobias uses
the fish's heart and liver to scare away the demon. At the request of his
new father-in-law, he stays with his new in-laws for several weeks and
his parents become concerned about his failure to return as planned.
Finally, Tobias and Sarah return to Tobit and Anna. They welcome the
couple home. Tobit's sight is restored through the salve made from the
fish's gall. Tobit tells Tobias to give his guide half of what he brought
back as a bonus for his safe return. Raphael calls the couple to instruct
them of righteous living. He then informs Sarah and Tobit that he is one
of the seven angels sent to answer their prayers and explains he was
only a vision. The angel, Raphael, returns to heaven.

Tobias has seven sons and his father dies at the age of 112. Before
Tobit's death, he encourages his family to move out of Nineveh to
Media before the prophecy that would scatter Israel and take some
into captivity. He tells Tobias the temple would be rebuilt and God
will restore Israel just as prophecy indicates. Tobias follows his
father's instructions, moves away from Nineveh and dies at 117
years old.

The Pentecost Connection

Remember, in Chapter 2, Tobit describes how a great dinner was prepared for him during the festival of weeks which he also describes as the festival of Pentecost in verse 1:

" . . . At our festival of Pentecost which is the sacred festival
of weeks . . . "

With this knowledge, we can now look at the scriptures found in Act 2: 1-13 in a different light. We now know that the Holy Spirit as described in the New Testament came on the day of the Jewish Festival of Weeks—Pentecost. We have uncovered that information because we chose to read the story of Tobit. If we examine the scriptures further, we will find additional details of why there was such a mixture of people described during both celebrations. In the Old Testament, the people are commanded to rejoice with strangers in Deuteronomy 16:11 as follows:

" . . . you and your sons and your daughters, your male and
female slaves, the Levites resident in your towns, as well as
the strangers, the orphans, and the widows who are among
you."

Therefore, it appears that the Jewish festival was being celebrated by the Jews in Acts 2 before the Holy Spirit broke loose among the people. Verse 5 confirms that Jews of every nation were present in Jerusalem at that time.

"Now there were devout Jews from every nation under heaven
living in Jerusalem." (Acts 2:5-11)

The Festival of Weeks was commanded by God in Deuteronomy 16 (the last book of the Torah). The description of the Festival of Weeks cannot be connected with Pentecost as translated in most Protestant Bibles. Here is how it is described in Deuteronomy 16: 9-10 and verse 16.

> 9. "You shall count seven weeks; begin to count the seven weeks from the time the sickle is first put to the standing grain. 10. Then you shall keep the festival of weeks to the Lord your God, contributing a freewill offering in proportion to the blessing that you have received from the Lord your God. 16. Three times a year all your males shall appear before the Lord your God at the place that he will choose: . . . at the festival of weeks, . . . They shall not appear before the Lord empty handed . . . " (NRSV)

In summary, the connection between the Festival of Weeks in the Old Testament and the Pentecost in the New Testament is brought together and better described from the story in the book of Tobit—a book that is not included in most Protestant Bibles.

Again, this is a fiction story. However, it describes potential trials, tribulations and blessings that can occur among God's people.

Book of
Judith

Introduction

This book is also fiction like the book of Tobit. Within the contents of the story, the writer mixes fictitious names and places with real names and places that existed during that period. The story line is very simple with only one inconsistency.

Summary

The main characters of this story are a woman named Judith and a man named Holofernes. Holofernes is seeking to capture the Israelites' city of Bethulia. He decides to seize all their springs and deprive them of water in hopes the Israelites will surrender without a fight. During this process, Holofernes beholds a beautiful Israelite woman named Judith. Holofernes begins to lust for her and makes plans to have intercourse with her. His plan is to get her drunk and have his way, but the tables are turned.

The widow woman, Judith, makes plans to meet him and makes plans to get Holofernes the drunkest he has ever been in his life. Once he becomes drunk and passes out on his bed, Judith cuts off his head and returns to her people. The people are surprised she survives and returns. They praise her for her heroic deed. The people put Holofernes' head on the wall and head to the Assyrians' camp. The Assyrians are surprised to see them and went to wake up Holofernes only to find his headless body. Holofernes' men scatter and are captured by the Israelites throughout the region and slaughtered.

The high priest of Joakim and Israel's elders who lived in Jerusalem came to thank Judith for what she had done and Judith is exalted among her people. Her hymn of praise is found in chapter 16.

There is one inconsistency in this story. In the first part of the story, the writer tells his readers that the enemies have guarded the Israelites water system so they can no longer draw out water for drinking and bathing. It has been completely rationed and there is no water left as stated in Chapter 7:21. Strangely enough, when Judith begins to put together her scheme to allure Holofernes with her beauty, she bathes before she goes. The writer fails to tell where Judith obtained her water. However, this contradiction does not take away the true purpose of this story.

This story describes how a faithful woman devotes herself to her people by conquering their oppressor through her intellect, physical bravery, and faith in God. Because of this, she becomes a hero and is admired and praised by her people. Most importantly, this story reminds people to "keep the faith" even during the most difficult of times.

Book of
Esther
with Additions

(The Greek Version Containing the Additional Chapters)

Introduction

The information in this book was originally written in Greek and added to the original book of Esther found in the Septuagint (The Septuagint is compiled of Hebrew Scriptures translated in the Greek language about 70 years before Christ is born. It is also known as the LXX). It is believed that this addition may have been written to compensate for an unaddressed issue in the originally written Hebrew text. As with any scripture, it is good to test the writings and assess its validity.

The Harper Collins Study Bible[3] found that the Greek text contains a more dramatic description of the king and his interaction with Esther at their first meeting than that of the Hebrew text. The Greek version considers the king's change of mind as moved from God in chapter 6:1 whereas the Hebrew text does not attribute this change to God.

---

[3]   *The Harper Collins Study Bible: New Revised Standard Version* Society of Biblical Literature. Harper San Francisco. Fulham Palace Road, London W6 8JB. 1989 (pg 1482)

(The Greek Version Containing the Additional Chapters)

Summary

This story begins with a dream of a man named Mordecai. This dream is quite similar to the symbolism used in Revelation. It follows:

> "Noises and confusion, thunders and earthquake, tumult on the earth! Then two great dragons came forward, both ready to fight and they roared terribly. At their roaring every nation prepared for war, to fight against the righteous nation. It was a day of darkness and gloom, of tribulation and distress, affliction and great tumult on the earth!" (Chapter 11:5-8)

In the book of Revelation, we find the same literary symbolism of a dragon used to represent evil in chapters 12, 13, 16, and 20. Both books were written almost within the same centuries (depending on your accepted date that Revelation was written). Therefore, the reader might view the use of these terms as a writing style of symbolism and not an apocalyptic reality through the existence of strange beasts.

After Mordecai has awakened from his dream, he desires to understand its meaning for the rest of the day. The writer's use of this dream provides an interesting introduction that summarizes the story for the reader through symbolism.

Following his dream, Mordecai uncovers two eunuchs plotting to kill the king and he reports them to King Artaxerxes. In return for the valued information, the King appoints Mordecai in his court and gives him many things for his loyalty.

As the story continues, the writer describes a special day whereupon a woman known as Queen Vashti is appointed to receive her diadem. However, she disobeys the king by refusing to accept it. Plans are made to find another beautiful and virtuous girl for the king. The king does not want a Jewish woman as his bride. However, in twelve months, Mordecai's foster daughter, Esther, is selected among all others to receive the diadem and become queen. She graciously accepts. Under the instructions of Mordecai, she remains quiet about being a devout Jew in her newly appointed role. She continues to secretly practice Jewish rituals and laws.

In the meantime, Mordecai continues to advance in the king's court and two more eunuchs became jealous of his advancement and makes plans to kill the king. Mordecai communicated this to Queen Esther who in turn communicates this to the king. A written memorial was left in the library to honor Mordecai for his kindness.

The king then gives a man named Haman a position of authority over all of his friends. This man expects all of the king's friends to curtsy before him and Mordecai refuses to do so. When he is questioned about his disobedience, he explains that he is a Jew. Haman becomes angry and wishes to destroy all the Jews. He proceeds to tell the king there is a certain nation that does not wish to keep his laws and offers to pay ten thousand talents of silver to destroy them. The king does not know that Mordecai is a Jew and is being set up to die. He allows Haman to send out a letter to the Jews explaining their future demise.

Upon hearing the news, Mordecai runs into the streets, rips his clothing, and puts on sackcloth. Esther's maids and eunuchs inform her of what happened. She sends a message to Mordecai and commands everyone to fast (including she and her maids). She declares she will go to the King and intercede for her people at the risk of being put to death for revealing her nationality.

Mordecai and Esther fast and pray. Esther is received by the king while Hamon plots to kill Mordecai. Esther tells the king of Haman's plot to kill the Jews while Haman is begging her for his life. The King becomes angry. Haman's plot to hang Mordecai fails, and Haman is hung in Mordecai's place. The king overrides the letters that Haman wrote to the Jews and Esther is given all the property that was owned by Haman.

The message of this story encourages the faithful to "keep the faith" and persevere during trials and tribulations.

Wisdom of Solomon

Introduction

The commentary in the Harper Collins Study Bible[4], writes that Solomon has been ruled out as the author by Bible scholars and the authorship of this book has been argued among scholars. However, I have looked beyond this unimportant issue because a disputed authorship does not affect the overall message that exists within the writings. Readers will reap sound and wise advice from this book and find several connections between the Old and New Testament and will also uncover a similar writing style that is found in the book of Revelation.

The writings evolve around the events that occurred after the existence of the Jewish monarchy. Since there is a wide range of topics covered in this book, I will focus on a few topics such as the writer's theory regarding length of life; love and characteristics of wisdom; and God the potter, bread of life, and deliverer.

As I wrote earlier, during the period this book was written, it is documented that the Greek culture and philosophy was rapidly growing and challenging many of the Jewish rituals and beliefs. In addition, the native Egyptians (an oppressor of the past) living in this area unjustly treat the Jews.

The estimated time period this book was written is between 250 B.C.E. and 50 C.E. The range is wide and overlaps into the period that the New Testament books were written. Throughout this summary, I

---

[4]   *The Harper Collins Study Bible: New Revised Standard Version.* Society of Biblical Literature. Harper San Francisco. Fulham Palace Road, London W6 8JB. 1989 (pg 1497)

will compare many of the similar writing styles in this book and in the New Testament books. Remember, the gospels were written between an estimated 50 C.E. to 110 C.E. The latter estimated date of the Book of Solomon falls into the period of the ministry of Jesus Christ and up to the writings of the New Testament books. Therefore, New Testament writers may have been influenced by some of these messages or writing styles.

Picture this—God delivers his nation from an oppressor that has brutally mistreated his people for many generations. After deliverance, God makes them a strong nation called Israel. They are ruled by a king and blessed with independence and prosperity. Their armies have conquered many other nations and their nation multiplies in people, possessions, and land. However, their prosperity drives many people away from faithful living and they begin to forget God's ways. After God has warned the people several times to repent of their sins, he allows them to be conquered by another nation and be taken into captivity once again! Years later, they come face-to-face with their ancestor's former oppressors—native Egyptians who team up with another nation to oppress them. How humbling would that be to a people called by God? As a believer of God, maybe you have had a similar humbling experience too. Remember these things as you read through the book.

Summary

Chapter 1: In the first chapter, the writer begins with what appears to be a sermon to the rulers about moral and immoral behavior. The rulers are encouraged to seek wisdom and turn to God. They are also asked to repent of their wickedness or they will be judged by God.

Chapter 2: The chapter follows with a description of how the wicked try to justify there is no hell and encourage people to enjoy life to the fullest, oppress the young ladies (verse 7 "let no flower of spring pass us by"), oppress the elderly, oppress the weak, and oppress the righteous. The writer describes how the wicked plot their actions of oppression in verses 12-20:

> ""Let us lie in wait for the righteous man, because he is inconvenient to us and opposes our actions; he reproaches us for sins against the law, and accuses us of sins against our training. He professes to have knowledge of God, and calls himself a child of the Lord. He became to us a reproof of our thoughts; the very sight of him is a burden to us, because his manner of life is unlike that of others, and his ways are strange. We are considered by him as something base, and he avoids our ways as unclean; he calls the last end of the righteous happy, and boasts that God is the father. Let us see if his words are true, and let us test what will happen at the end of his life; for if the righteous man is God's child, he will help him, and will deliver him from the hand of his adversaries. Let us test him with insult and torture, so that we may find

out how gentle he is, and make trial of his forbearance. Let us
condemn him to a shameful death, for, according to what he
says, he will be protected.""

And the writer replies to their plans in verses 21-24:

"Thus they reasoned, but they were led astray, for their
wickedness blinded them, and they did not know the secret
purposes of God, nor hoped for the wages of holiness, nor
discerned the prize for blameless souls; for God created us for
incorruption, and made us in the image of his own eternity,
but through the devil's envy death entered the world, and
those who belong to his company experience it."

All of these analogies describe the value of life and theory of life
and after-life among the wicked until verse 21. In verse 23, the writer
then comments how the oppressor is blinded by their sins and that the
earthly death of the righteous is the beginning of eternal life with God
who is "the image of his own eternity"

Chapter 3: The writer describes how the cold-hearted wickedness of
the oppressor does not seek to console those who have lost loved ones
or whose lives are in danger. It is written that in the eyes of the wicked,
the death of the righteous is not a tragedy although the wicked make that
determination. In order to get his point across, the writer provides an
analogy that describes how these difficulties build faith as follows:

"Having been disciplined a little, they will receive great good,
because God tested them and found them worthy of himself;
like gold" *(faith)* "in the furnace he tried them . . . " (verses 5
and 6)

This same analogy is also found in the book of Revelation in chapter 3 verse 18 and follows:

"Therefore I counsel you to buy from me gold" *(faith)* "refined by fire so that you may be rich"

In addition, another similar analogy of faith with the same cause and affect can be found in 1 Peter 1:7

"so that the genuineness of your faith-being more precious than gold that, though perishable, is tested by fire—may be found to result in praise and glory and honor when Jesus Christ is revealed."

This writing style provides us with a connection of ministry and thought between the Apocrypha and New Testament.

At this point, we have identified how God's people suffered persecution before the New Testament church is established. The people are being warned that persecution is probable and it will strengthen their faith and testimony.

The book of Sirach that follows the Widsom of Solomon will give us more details of how persecution existed prior to the birth of Jesus Christ and how it began to escalate as the Greek society became more powerful. For more understanding of how such conditions progressed, I have inserted a commentary for Matthew 4:23-25 during the time of Jesus:

"The elite supported itself on the backs of the poor! Hunger, malnutrition, poor hygiene, hard work," and "anxiety mean poor health. Demon possession, in which demons invade the body reflects invasive political, military, and economic control.[5]"

The commentary injects some wisdom into describing the conditions that prepares the way for the ministry of Jesus—the great physician and his new kingdom. In Luke 4:18, Jesus tells the people that he is there to heal them and bring "good news" to the poor and enslaved. He reads this message from Isaiah 61:1.

Length of Life

A long life to those who obey their parents is promised in Exodus 20:12. However, as we enter into this time period, we now note a change of thought occurring around the length of one's life. The writer theorizes that a shortened life of the oppressed under the hands of their oppressor is a final act of eternal peace. This is described in chapter 4 verses 7-19 as follows:

> "But the righteous, though they die early, will be at rest. For old age is not honored for length of time, or measured by number of years; but understanding is gray hair for anyone, and a blameless life is ripe old age. There were some who pleased God and were loved by him, and while living among sinners were taken up. They were caught up so that evil might not change their understanding or guile deceive their souls. For the fascination of wickedness obscures what is good, and roving desire perverts the innocent mind. Being perfected in a short time, they fulfilled long years; for their souls were pleasing to the Lord, therefore he took them quickly from the midst of

---

[5]   *The New Interpreter's Study Bible: New Revised Standard Version with the Apocrypha.* Abingdon Press. Nashville, TN (pg 1754)

wickedness. Yet the peoples saw and did not understand, or take such a thing to heart, that God's grace and mercy are with his elect, and that he watches over his holy ones."

Love and Characteristics of Wisdom

In chapter 6, the writer explains how important wisdom is and once again communicates this to the kings. Chapters 7, 8, and 9 describe how Solomon, the past king, embraced wisdom and valued it among all things. He enjoyed it, and obtained it throughout his life. It was so important to him that he asked for it in prayer at a young age. His prayers are found within these three chapters.

Chapter 10 begins with a description of how wisdom empowered Adam to rule and act as his deliverer from sin. He describes how Caleb's reluctance to bond with wisdom was the result of his downfall. He also describes all other things wisdom has done to rescue the righteous and the negative outcome of wickedness. In chapter 11, the writer picks up on analyzing how God and wisdom worked in the events that occurred after Solomon and reminds his people how wisdom guided the Israelites during their journey in the desert and looked after their needs. At the end of this chapter, the writer describes how God destroyed the wicked and reminds the people of the power of God's love, mercy, and forgiveness. This is the general thought repeated throughout the remainder of the chapter.

GOD: The Potter, The Bread of Life, The Deliverer

In chapter 16, the writer consoles the faithful by reminding them of the positive outcome of worshipping the "True God," whose love and desire to skillfully form us for his glory just as a potter forms clay for his delight. At the end of the chapter, he returns to describing the vanity of those who worship idols and again recalls the blessings of a providing God who delivered the Israelites from many things as they traveled through the desert. Then in verse 26, he writes a message, encouraging the people to seek God's word much like the style of message communicated to the people by Jesus:

> "so that your children, whom you loved, O Lord, might learn
> that it is not the production of crops that feeds humankind but
> that your word sustains those who trust in you."

Compare this to Jesus words in Matthew 4:4 when he was tempted by Satan as he fasted:

> ""One does not live by bread alone, but by every word that
> comes from the mouth of God."" (NRSV)

In addition, Jesus states in John 6:48
""I am the bread of life.""

As I wrote before, this period is either setting the foundation for the birth of Jesus and the New Testament church or embracing the message of Christ.

In chapter 17, the writer returns to the events of Israel's deliverance from the Egyptians, and as he moves into chapter 18, the writer begins to write an account of how the death of the Egyptians' firstborn affected them in verse 5. This is not found in most Protestant Old Testament Bibles and provides insight into the Egyptians' anger that manifested from what happened to their first born. It describes the horror of massive death that occurred among the Egyptians. This provides further insight into why the Egyptians teamed up with the Greek society to oppress the Jews—they sought cold-hearted revenge. This problem is not strongly captured in the New Testament.

In his last and final verse, he concludes his book with praise to God to glorify him for all things he has done for the people and meeting their needs during their time of hardships.

The important message in this book supports faith in God, provides a perspective of the unfaithful, and also encourages perseverance and hope through trials and tribulations among the faithful reminding the people to keep the faith because God will exalt and glorify them and meet their needs. It also sets the stage for the ministry of Jesus or embraces the message of Jesus depending on the date it was written.

Book of
Ecclesiasticus, or
the Wisdom of Jesus
Son of Sirach

Book of Ecclesiasticus, or the Wisdom of Jesus Son of Sirach

Introduction

According to an NRSV[6] commentary, this book was read by young scholars that were being schooled somewhere between 200 and 180 B.C.E. It was during this period the Seleucids (those who reigned after Alexander the Great in Antioch) grappled for control over Judea which was ruled by the Ptolemies of Egypt. The social setting for this period hinges around the conflict between the Ptolemies and Seleucids seeking to control and threaten the existence of the Jewish culture and its teachings. Sirach tries to instill the social values and principles of Jewish teachings found throughout the Torah (The Torah is known to Protestants as the first five books of the Old Testament which is also referred as the Pentateuch.) The book reiterates most social values that need to be practiced in a believer's daily life. It contains good information for anyone who is seeking ethical and moral values.

Its unique format begins with a prologue written by the grandson of Sirach. The grandson embraces learning and the importance of communicating learned theological and historical facts through much study of the books of "our ancestors." In the prologue, Sirach's grandson states that the contents of these books which have been translated several times throughout the years may have lost some of their original meaning. Any of us who have studied history realize that a word's meaning and

---

[6]   *The Harper Collins Study Bible: New Revised Standard Version.* Society of Biblical Literature. Harper San Francisco. Fulham Palace Road, London W6 8JB. 1989

slang can change throughout generations; therefore, the grandson of Sirach's statement confirms that scripture accuracy **can be questioned** based on changing times and human error. This statement may raise some eyebrows among certain Christians today.

The argument of indifference among Christians may generate among those that believe each word is perfectly inspired and written through the guidance of the Holy Spirit. They may label such a statement made by the grandson of Sirach as blasphemous. However, to other Christians, a statement like this confirms the reality of human error as well as the affects of generational language and cultural changes that reinforce discernment through faith and a personal relationship with God.

Today, the troubling times of our 21st century contain many of the same social issues as discussed during Sirach's time. Many readers may find his words of wisdom comforting and a source of guidance in their day-to-day life situations. As during the time of Sirach, it is important that Christians also become thoroughly educated in their understanding of theological history which is of the utmost importance in understanding the Bible. Although some theologians question the validity of some text, I find a foundation of truth and comfort threaded throughout the contents of the book of Sirach and the Bible that reinforces a God connection.

Since there is so much information in this book, I will summarize verses in chapters containing topics on the poor, friendship, loaning, counsel, overeating, and physicians. There are other interesting topics in this book that require further study.

Book of Ecclesiasticus, or the Wisdom of Jesus Son of Sirach

Summary

Chapter 4

This chapter outlines the duties to the poor and oppressed. During this period of time, we have learned that the Jews faced the same economic problems of poverty we face today. The writer does not suggest that the needs of the poor be ignored. In fact, there are several chapters within this book outlining the merciful process of dealing with such conditions. He advises the people to meet the needs of the poor, abstain from cheating them, and/or keep them in waiting for assistance. If they treat the poor unjustly, the writer warns them that the "Creator" will hear the prayers of the poor. According to The Harper Collins Study Bible[7], this particular set of instructions were given to students who were studying law. However, this same message can be applied today toward all Christians in support of social justice.

Chapter 6

Backstabbing people have been around for centuries. In today's world, it is not hard to find backstabbers within our social realm. Therefore, life quickly teaches us to be on guard and choose our friends carefully. As I described in the introduction, during the time this book was written, the Jewish people were up against much conflict. (You will learn about the

---

[7] *The Harper Collins Study Bible: New Revised Standard Version.* Society of Biblical Literature. Harper San Francisco. Fulham Palace Road, London W6 8JB. 1989

backstabbing tactics of the enemy in I and II Maccabees.) The advice given to the Jewish people during this period can also be applied to today's social issues. The moral minority must stand strong against a growing culture that may not always share the same convictions and moral values

Have you ever experienced an insincere friendship with a professed believer? Throughout history and today, many professing Christians fight, backstab, and oppress other Christians and people. That is why the author encourages his readers to exercise great caution in testing of friends. We must weed out the unworthy and maintain the "best friends forever" as described in Chapter 6.verses 5-17.

The author begins this chapter by informing us that "pleasant speech" will increase the amount of friends we have and if we watch our manners, then we will open the door to the kind consideration of others. This is common sense and many of us have been told to watch our manners since we were little children. However, the author takes this a little further and warns us to be selective in choosing our friends because some people will not support us during times of difficulties. Certain types of friends may backstab us and become our foes. They will tell others about our difficulties or arguments to embarrass us. Although they may dine with us, they will not support us when we are facing difficulties or have been humbled. Be careful of these types of friends because as long as we are flourishing they will always be there like our shadow, but when we experience troubling times, they will become our enemy and avoid us.

What is a faithful friend? The author answers this question in verses 14-17. He describes a true friend as "shelter, treasure, priceless", and "life-saving medicine", and he encourages his students to obtain friends who also embrace wisdom.

I will quickly move forward to chapter 37 to include an additional chapter that has a similar message. The author describes the deceit and backstabbing of an insincere friend.

Chapter 37

Verses 1-6: Beware of False Friends.

> "Every friend says, "I too am a friend"; but some friends are friends only in name. Is it not a sorrow like that for death itself when a dear friend turns into an enemy? O inclination to evil, why were you formed to cover the land with deceit? Some companions rejoice in the happiness of a friend, but in time of trouble they are against him. Some companions help a friend for their stomachs' sake, yet in battle they will carry his shield. Do not forget a friend during the battle, and do not be unmindful of him when you distribute your spoils." (NRSV)

Returning back to Chapter 6, the author describes why wisdom is such an important attribute in the friends we choose.

Verse 36-37—wisdom and the importance of association with the likes.

He informs his readers that when you observe someone who is very wise, you need to make every effort to get up early and "let your foot wear out his doorstep[8]." However, as you are seeking their wisdom, continue to ponder on the laws of the Lord and reflect on them constantly. " . . . he will give insight to your mind, and your desire for wisdom will be granted[9]."

---

[8]   *The Harper Collins Study Bible: New Revised Standard Version.* Society of Biblical Literature. Harper San Francisco. Fulham Palace Road, London W6 8JB. 1989

[9]   *The Harper Collins Study Bible: New Revised Standard Version.* Society of Biblical Literature. Harper San Francisco. Fulham Palace Road, London W6 8JB. 1989

Chapter 8

The writer informs his students how to handle their relationships with the wealthy, the powerful, and intellectual elders among them. This advice is extremely pertinent in making good choices in social relationships and can just as fairly be applied and taught today.

In chapter 8, the author gives us a list of things we should not do. He informs us to be careful when we dispute with individuals of higher economic or political power because their influence may prevail over our well-being and justice. He reminds his readers that wealth and politics has ruined the moral values of many leaders. Be careful and abstain from disputing with the "loud mouth" and do not aggravate their angry outrage. Do not laugh at someone who is ill-bred because one of your own relatives may be insulted. Do not dishonor a person who has repented of sin because we have all sinned and are worthy of discipline. Do not hate someone who is old or rejoice over death. By all means, some of us will grow old; and all of us are destined to die. Learn from the sages and laws so that you may serve the leaders. Learn and respect the elderly who have gained knowledge from their parents. Do not irritate angry or rude people because they may "bring you to your feet[10]" and you may be trapped. Do not lend to a person who is stronger than you, or you may have to write off the debt. Do not accept liability for another person's debt. If you do, be ready to pay it. Do not take a judge to court; the final verdict will be influenced by his political position. Do not go on a trip with the irresponsible. They will oppress you with their carelessness and in their madness you may die with them. Do not start an argument with the hot-blooded or take a trip with them into the

---

[10] *The Harper Collins Study Bible: New Revised Standard Version.* Society of Biblical Literature. Harper San Francisco. Fulham Palace Road, London W6 8JB. 1989

unpopulated areas because they may murder you—life is of no value to them and there is nobody there to plead for your life. Do not disclose secretes or seek advice from unwise people. Unwise people will not guard your secretes. Cautiously secure your secretes from all strangers.

Chapter 11—Again, the writer informs his students how to interact with others and the importance of being humble in verses 1-9. At this point, I find the writer's words so carefully chosen and difficult to paraphrase. From this point forward, I will quote from The Harper Collins Study Bible: NRSV.

Interacting with Other People—Some Things to Ponder

> "The wisdom of the humble lifts their heads high, and seats them among the great. Do not praise individuals for their good looks, or loathe anyone because of appearance alone. The bee is small among flying creatures, but what it produces is the best of sweet things. Do not boast about wearing fine clothes, and do not exalt yourself when you are honored; for the works of the Lord are wonderful, and his works are concealed from humankind."

When in a position to analyze the actions of others, take head to the following advice found in verses 7-9:

> "Do not find fault before you investigate: examine first, and then criticize. Do not answer before you listen, and do not interrupt when another is speaking. Do not argue about a matter that does not concern you, and do not sit with sinners when they judge a case."

Chapter 12
Verses 8-18—a word on enemies

"A friend is not known in prosperity, nor is an enemy hidden
in adversity. One's enemies are friendly when one prospers,
but in adversity even one's friend disappears. Never trust your
enemy, for like corrosion in copper, so is his wickedness. Even
if he humbles himself and walks bowed down, take care to be
on your guard against him. Be to him like one who polishes
a mirror, to be sure it does not become completely tarnished.
Do not put him next to you, or he may overthrow you and
take your place. Do not let him sit at your right hand, or else
he may try to take your own seat, and at last you will realize
the truth of my words, and be stung by what I have said. Who
pities a snake charmer when he is bitten, or all those who go
near wild animals? So no one pities a person who associates
with a sinner and becomes involved in other's sins. He stands
by you for a while, but if you falter, he will not be there. An
enemy speaks sweetly with his lips, but in his heart he plans to
throw you into a pit; an enemy may have tears in his eyes, but
if he finds an opportunity he will never have enough of your
blood. If evil comes upon you, you will find him there ahead
of you; pretending to help, he will trip you up. Then he will
shake his head, and clap his hands, and whisper much, and
show his true face."

Chapter 13

This chapter discusses establishing relationships with rich people.
The writer is warning the reader to be careful with whom they associate
with in their public dealings. The commentary in the New Interpreter's

Study Bible indicates that the two classes of upper and lower class did not peacefully socialize with each other during this period. If a poor person from the lower class dared to socialize with a wealthy person, they ran the risk of being degraded and unethically used and oppressed. According to the commentary, the wealthy are associated with the intellect and the lower class (I assume are the poor and uneducated) are defined as oppressed[11]. Here is what Sirach has to say about the wealthy in verses 1-7:

"Whoever touches pitch gets dirty, and whoever associates with a proud person becomes like him." (According to the commentary in The Harper Collins Study Bible, the first part of this verse is a proverb that can be traced from Theognis, to Sirach, to Shakespeare, and to the present day[12].)

"Do not lift a weight too heavy for you, or associate with one mightier and richer than you. How can the clay pot associate with the iron kettle? The pot will strike against it and be smashed. A rich person does wrong, and even adds insults; a poor person suffers wrong, and must add apologies. A rich person will exploit you if you can be of use to him, but if you are in need he will abandon you. If you own something, he will live with you; he will drain your resources without a qualm. When he needs you he will deceive you, and will smile at you and encourage you; he will speak to you kindly

---

[11] *The New Interpreter's Study Bible: New Revised Standard Version with the Apocrypha.* Abingdon Press. Nashville, TN 1989 (page 1469)

[12] *The Harper Collins Study Bible: New Revised Standard Version.* Society of Biblical Literature. Harper San Francisco. Fulham Palace Road, London W6 8JB. 1989 (page 1551)

and say, "What do you need?" He will embarrass you with his delicacies, until he has drained you two or three times, and finally he will laugh at you. Should he see you afterwards, he will pass you by and shake his head at you.

As we continue on with this chapter, I would like to share the commentary found in the New Interpreter's Bible[13]. This information gives us some understanding as to why the writer of Sirach might be conveying the differences between the poor and wealthy and how the Greek laws and ideas contradicted Jewish culture.

"The Hellenization of the Near East had already taken hold among the educated upper classes by the time Ben Sira put his teachings into writing. It appears that many Jews were wondering whether their ancient traditions could match the comprehensiveness and depth of Greek thought. Being a well-traveled man, Ben Sira would have witnessed the decline in fervor that had overtaken many of his fellow Jews. Being an observant Jew, he would have been greatly troubled by this decline. It seems clear that his object in writing was to show the Jews of his day that real wisdom was to be found in the traditions of Israel and not in Greek philosophy. He intended his work to be comprehensive, authoritative reference wherein could be found guidance and instruction for every circumstance of life."

Caring for the poor was not embraced in the Greek philosophy. A commentary for Matthew 4:23-25 gives us further information indicating

[13] *The New Interpreter's Study Bible: New Revised Standard Version with the Apocrypha.* Abingdon Press. Nashville, TN 1989 (page 1451)

that although the Romans boasted of the great health, their rural peasants (which made up most of the population) were harshly overtaxed by Rome, their cities, rich landowners, and of all things, Jerusalem's priests. Therefore, the highly privileged citizens were supported by its poor. This type of behavior is not in line with God's social order. With this in mind, let us continue with the following proverbs from verse 15 to 26:

"Every creature loves its like, and every person the neighbor. All living beings associate with their own kind, and people stick close to those like themselves. What does a wolf have in common with a lamb? No more has a sinner with the devout. What peace is there between a hyena and a dog? And what peace between the rich and the poor? Wild asses in the wilderness are the prey of lions; likewise the poor are feeding grounds for the rich. Humility is an abomination to the proud; likewise the poor are an abomination to the rich. When the rich person totters, he is supported by friends, but when the humble falls, he is pushed away even by friends. If the rich person slips, many come to the rescue; he speaks unseemly words, but they justify him. If the humble person slips, they even criticize him; he talks sense, but is not given a hearing. The rich person speaks and all are silent; they extol to the clouds what he says. The poor person speaks and they say, "Who is this fellow?" And should he stumble, they even push him down. Riches are good if they are free from sin; poverty is evil only in the opinion of the ungodly. The heart changes the countenance, either for good or for evil. The sign of a happy heart is a cheerful face, but to devise proverbs requires painful thinking."

In the previous text, in verses 15-26 of chapter 13, the writer of Sirach is showing the contrasting difference between Jewish and Greek social laws. Through his analogy, he is describing how their differences place a wedge between the two societies.

In verse 1-19 of the following chapter, the writer of Sirach provides justification for following God's social laws and describes the negative impact Greek laws have on society.

Chapter 14
Verses 1-19: proper management and use of wealth

"Happy are those who do not blunder with their lips, and need not suffer remorse for sin. Happy are those whose hearts do not condemn them, and who have not given up their hope. Riches are inappropriate for a small-minded person; and of what use is wealth to a miser? What he denies himself he collects for others; and others will live in luxury on his goods. If one is mean to himself, to whom will he be generous? He will not enjoy his own riches. No one is worse than one who is grudging to himself; this is the punishment for his meanness. If ever he does good, it is by mistake; and in the end he reveals his meanness. The miser is an evil person; he turns away and disregards people. The eye of the greedy person is not satisfied with his share; greedy injustice withers the soul. A miser begrudges bread, and it is lacking at his table. My child, treat yourself well, according to your means, and present worthy offerings to the Lord. Remember that death does not tarry, and the decree of Hades has not been shown to you. Do good to friends before you die, and reach out and give to them as much as you can. Do not deprive yourself of a day's enjoyment; do not let your share of desired good pass by you. Will you not leave the fruit of your labors to another, and what you acquired by toil to be divided by lot? Give, and take, and indulge yourself, because in Hades one cannot look for luxury. All living beings become old like a garment, for the decree from of old is "You must die!" Like abundant leaves on a spreading tree that sheds some and puts forth others, so are the generations of flesh and blood: one dies and another is born. Every work decays and ceases to exist, and the one who made it will pass away with it."

Chapter 29

The principles and concepts of loaning and borrowing are described in this chapter. Sirach provides some good tips in helping the poor. During these difficult economic times of the 21st century, many of God's people have forgotten how to justly care for others. They fail to reach out to those who are struggling financially and prefer to label them losers instead of kindly offering them some help to get on their feet again.

The concepts found in Sirach are not embraced by our American banking institutions either. We live in a period when interest rates on loans, especially periodically adjusted mortgages and credit cards, have skyrocketed so high they have created oppressive conditions that force homeowners into foreclosure and financially bankrupt others. If the principles found in this chapter were applied to today's banking procedures, banks would not have experienced such loan losses from overburdened consumers who were so financially strapped they could not make good on their loans.

On the other hand, we live in a time where some people who have the funds to pay their creditors refuse to pay back the loaned money. This is addressed in Sirach as well.

Much of the advice that Sirach offers within this chapter can also be found in the Old Testament and New Testament. These principles are important ways for a financial institution and consumer to conduct business. Before, I share the scriptures found in chapter 29, I would like to share other scriptures found in the Old and New Testament that support Sirach's words of wisdom. The first source being found in Proverbs 22: 7-9 and 22-27 follows:

> "The rich rule over the poor, and the borrower is the slave of the lender. Whoever sows injustice will reap calamity, and the rod of anger will fail. Those who are generous are blessed, for they share their bread with the poor." (verses 7-9)

> "Do not rob the poor because they are poor, or crush the afflicted at the gate; for the Lord pleads their cause and despoils of life those who despoil them . . . Do not be one of those who give pledges, who become surety for debts. If you have nothing with which to pay, why should your bed be taken from under you?" (verses 22-27 from NRSV)

In addition to the above verses, the following verses can be found in the New Testament regarding the treatment of those in need and follows:

> "How does God's love abide in anyone who has the world's goods and sees a brother or sister in need and yet refuses help?." (1 John 3:17)

> "Love does no wrong to a neighbor; therefore, love is the fulfilling of the law." (Romans 13:10)

Sirach has a lot to say about lending, borrowing, and the treatment of the poor in chapter 29 as well as encouraging respect between lender and recipient. Twenty verses of advice are devoted to this issue. The first set of advice is found in verses 1-7.

In this section, the writer makes two points of expectations before issuing a warning to the lender. First, if you follow the commandments, you will have compassion for your neighbors and assist them in their times of need. Secondly, if money has been loaned to you, you must pay it back to your neighbor as agreed upon.

Now, the author issues a warning to the compassionate neighbor. He warns them that some people may consider a loan as unexpected gain to squander as they wish. Prior to receiving the loan, you may be treated with great kindness and once they have received the loan from you, they will renege on making payments as promised. Their payments will not be made to you as expected or you may be paid back half of what is owed to you. At this point, you will consider whatever funds they pay you as financial gain. If the irresponsible person does not pay back the money as promised, they have plundered you, severed your friendship, and made them your foe. He concludes that for this reason, many compassionate neighbors are hesitant to lend.

In verses 8-14, the writer advises us to immediately help individuals in poverty. The author again reminds his readers that this is the commandment. Do not send the poverty stricken individuals away without help. Give up your silver and worldly wealth least it become corroded or destroyed. Care for your relatives and friends, and build up your wealth as decreed by "the most High." Charity will rescue you and grant you safety from your foe. A kind person will not fail their neighbor and will meet their needs, but a uncaring person will certainly fail his neighbor.

Sirach's advice reminds me of the story of a very rich man named Zacchaeus found in Luke 19:8. As children, many of us sang the song of how he watched Jesus while sitting in a tree. All of us learned that he was a short man and a sinner that was transformed after meeting Jesus.

However, another important point that is lost in that story is how he gave half of his goods to the poor upon his transformation. Half of his goods! His transformed heart did not stop at giving half of his goods to the poor, but also convicted him to promise anyone that he deceitfully obtained money from a repayment of four times the amount he overcharged them. He sought to obey the commandments of God by investing his wealth in the Kingdom of God.

Verses 15-20: informs individuals to respect those who lend to them and warns lenders to be cautious in lending.

The author concludes this section with a final summary of lending practices as follow:

> "Do not forget the kindness of your guarantor, for he has given his life for you. A sinner wastes the property of his guarantor, and the ungrateful person abandons his rescuer. Being surety has ruined many who were prosperous, and has tossed them about like waves of the sea; it has driven the influential into exile, and they have wandered among foreign nations. The sinner comes to grief through surety; his pursuit of gain involves him in lawsuits. Assist your neighbor to the best of your ability, but be careful not to fall yourself."

(According to The Study Bible Commentary, the word "life" in the above text does not reference the human form, but in the form of "property or livelihood.[14]*")*

---

[14]   *The Harper Collins Study Bible: New Revised Standard Version*. Society of Biblical Literature. Harper San Francisco. Fulham Palace Road, London W6 8JB. 1989

Verses 21-28: the essential things in life

Anyone who has studied psychology will find that verse 21 contains a familiar theory of human needs. In Maslow's hierarchy theory, which was developed in 1943, the three elements listed in verse 21 are described as essential needs in the first level of Maslow's pyramid. However, Sirach mentions a need for a house and Maslow mentions a need for sleep. Maybe the lack of sleep was not a problem during Sirach's time. Sirach's essential needs for life follow:

> "The necessities of life are water, bread, and clothing, and also a house to assure privacy. Better is the life of the poor under their own crude roof than sumptuous food in the house of others. Be content with little or much, and you will hear no reproach for being a guest. It is a miserable life to go from house to house; as a guest you should not open your mouth; you will play the host and provide drink without being thanked, and besides this you will hear rude words like these: "Come here, stranger, prepare the table; let me eat what you have there." "Be off, stranger, for an honored guest is here; my brother has come for a visit, and I need the guest-room." It is hard for a sensible person to bear scolding about lodging and the insults of the moneylender."

Chapter 33

VERSES 1-15: God's creation and predestination.

In this chapter, Sirach uses the same analogy that Jeremiah and Isaiah use to describe how God (as the potter) forms his people (the clay) into what he desires. This analogy suggests that God has a predestined plan for our lives. Once we have exercised our free-will in our decision making process, God may need to do a little work in us as described

in the potter and the clay story. We find this molding analogy of God's
power to occur among individuals, nations, and creations in other parts
of the Bible. The first clay analogy that I have quoted comes from the
book of Isaiah addressing an individual:

> " . . . Shall the potter be regarded as the clay? Shall the
> thing made say of its maker, "He did not make me"; or
> the thing formed say of the one who formed it, "He has no
> understanding"?" (Isaiah 29:16)

> "Yet, O Lord, you are our Father; we are the clay, and you are
> our potter; we are all the work of your hand." (Isaiah 64:8)

The second clay analogy that I am referring to is found in the book of
Jeremiah and is used to describe a nation:

> "The word that came to Jeremiah from the Lord: "Come,
> go down to the potter's house, and there I will let you hear
> my words." So I went down to the potter's house, and there
> he was working at his wheel. The vessel he was making of
> clay was spoiled in the potter's hand, and he reworked it into
> another vessel, as seemed good to him. Then the word of the
> Lord came to me; Can I not do with you, O house of Israel,
> just as the potter has done? Says the Lord. Just like the clay in
> the potter's hand, so are you in my hand, O house of Israel. At
> one moment I may declare concerning a nation or a kingdom,
> that I will pluck up and break down and destroy it, but if that
> nation, concerning which I have spoken, turns from its evil,
> I will change my mind about the disaster that I intended to
> bring on it. And at another moment I may declare concerning a

nation or a kingdom that I will build and plant it, but if it does evil in my sight, not listening to my voice, then I will change my mind about the good that I have intended to do to it. Now, therefore, say to the people of Judah and the inhabitants of Jerusalem: Thus says the Lord: Look, I am a potter shaping evil against you and devising a plan against you. Turn now, all of you from your evil way, and amend your ways and your doings." (Jeremiah 18:1-11)

Sirach's analogy began with a powerful God in charge of the individuals and nations then extends to God's power over all creation in 33: 7-13:

"Why is one day more important than another, when all the daylight in the year is from the sun? By the Lord's wisdom they were distinguished, and he appointed the different seasons and festivals. Some days he exalted and hallowed, and some he made ordinary days. All human beings come from the ground, and humankind was created out of the dust. In the fullness of his knowledge the Lord distinguished them and appointed their different ways. Some he blessed and exalted, and some he made holy and brought near to himself; but some he cursed and brought low, and turned them out of their place. Like clay in the hand of the potter, to be molded as he pleases, so all are in the hand of their Maker, to be given whatever he decides."

The New Testament also includes such an analogy in Romans 9:11-21. The writer of Romans also describes how God's plan is not always our plan as in the case of Jacob and Esau. Remember the story of the two brothers? According to Jewish law, Esau (the first-born) was in line for the blessing, however, God took the last-born (Jacob) and made him the greatest of the two by allowing him to receive the blessing. The message is summed up as God is the potter, we are the clay. He will mold us as God chooses and not always as we expect and/or according to our human understanding, ritual, and practices.

Even before they had been born or had done anything good or bad (so that God's purpose of election might continue, not by works but by his call) she was told, "The elder shall serve the younger." . . . So it depends not on human will or exertion, but on God who shows mercy. For the scripture says to Pharaoh, "I have raised you up for the very purpose of showing my power in you, so that my name may be proclaimed in all the earth." So then he has mercy on whomever he chooses, and he hardens the heart of whomever he chooses. You will say to me then, "Why then does he still find fault? For who can resist his will?" But who indeed are you, a human being, to argue with God? Will what is molded say to the one who molds it, "Why have you made me like this?" Has the potter no right over the clay, to make out of the same lump one object for special use and another for ordinary use?"

In addition to those Jews who were also listening to this message found in Romans, the writer adds in verses 27-29:

"And Isaiah cries out concerning Israel, "Though the number of the children of Israel were like the sand of the sea, only a remnant of them will be saved; for the Lord will execute his sentence on the earth quickly and decisively." And as Isaiah predicted, "If the Lord of hosts had not left survivors to us, we would have fared like Sodom and been made like Gomorrah.""""

A message of hope for Israel radiates in Isaiah, Jeremiah, Sirach and Romans. It is a message confirming that many Jews may not survive exiles, battles, and persecution, but God has appointed a remnant to remain. This prophecy remains true today. These four books suggest that all things come to pass for a purpose, and the book of Sirach assists in reiterating that all people and nations are under the work and power of God. He is the potter; we are the clay.

CHAPTER 37

In this section, the author stresses the importance of seeking wise counsel and discriminating between good and bad judgment. Again, I will directly quote the author's carefully chosen words.

Verses 7-15: cautiously seek advice

"All counselors praise the counsel they give, but some give counsel in their own interest. Be wary of a counselor, and learn first what is his interest, for he will take thought for himself. He may cast the lot against you and tell you, "Your way is good," and then stand aside to see what happens to you. Do not consult the one who regards you with suspicion; hide your intentions from those who are jealous of you. Do not consult with a woman about her rival or with a coward about war, with a merchant about business or with a buyer about selling, with a miser about generosity or with the merciless about kindness, with an idler about any work or with a seasonal laborer about completing his work, with a lazy servant about a big task—pay no attention to any advice they give. "But associate with a godly person whom you know to be a keeper of the commandments, who is like-minded with yourself, and who will grieve with you if you fail. And heed the counsel of your own heart, for no one is more faithful to you than it is. For our own mind sometimes keeps us better informed than seven sentinels sitting high on a watchtower. But above all pray to the most High that he may direct your way in truth."

Verses 16-26: discerning good and bad judgment

"Discussion is the beginning of every work, and counsel precedes every undertaking. The mind is the root of all conduct; it sprouts four branches, good and evil, life and death; and it is the tongue that continually rules them. Some people may be clever enough to teach many, and yet be useless to themselves. A skillful speaker may be hated; he will be destitute of all food, for the Lord has withheld the gift of charm, since he is lacking in all wisdom. If a person is wise to his own advantage, the fruits of his good sense will be praiseworthy. A wise person instructs his own people, and the fruits of his good sense will endure. A wise person will have praise heaped upon him, and all who see him will call him happy. The days of a person's life are numbered, but the days of Israel are without number. One who is wise among his people will inherit honor, and his name will live forever."

Notice that the days of Israel's people are with number in the last part of the above paragraph, but the nation of Israel is not numbered. The Apocrypha supports God's promise to Israel and reflects the deep-seeded confirmation of hope and faith grounded in the heart of a Jew.

Last but not least, the last five verses of this chapter support doing everything in moderation and encourage the reader to refrain from over-indulgence and gluttony. As many Americans know, the effects of being overweight can cause many illnesses and health problems. The writer communicates this to his reader in verses 27-31 before he further discusses health and doctor concerns in the next chapter.

"My child, test yourself while you live; see what is bad for you and do not give in to it. For not everything is good for everyone, and no one enjoys everything. Do not be greedy for every delicacy, and do not eat without restraint; for overeating brings sickness, and gluttony leads to nausea. Many have died of gluttony, but the one who guards against it prolongs his life."

Chapter 38:

Verses 1 through 15 support the work of God-fearing, wise doctors. If this verse was included within the scriptures of all Protestant's Bible, would denominations that refuse medical treatment exist? In this scripture, the writer fully supports the use of medical doctors within the text of these fifteen verses which are worthy to be quoted and follow:

"Honor physicians for their services, for the Lord created them; for their gift of healing comes from the Most High, and they are rewarded by the king. The skill of physicians makes them distinguished, and in the presence of the great they are admired. The Lord created medicines out of the earth, and the sensible will not despise them. Was not water made sweet with a tree in order that its power might be known? And he gave skill to human beings that he might be glorified in his marvelous works. By them the physician heals and takes away pain; the pharmacist makes a mixture from them. God's works will never be finished; and from him health spreads over all the earth. My child, when you are ill, do not delay, but pray to the Lord, and he will heal you. Give up your faults and direct your hands rightly, and cleanse your heart from all sin. Offer a sweet-smelling sacrifice, and a memorial portion of choice flour, and pour oil on your offering, as much as you can afford. Then give the physician his place, for the Lord created him; do not let him leave you, for you need him. There may come a time when recovery lies in the hands of physicians, for they too pray to the Lord that he grant them success in diagnosis and in healing, for the sake of preserving life. He who sins against his Maker, will be defiant toward the physician."

The writer of this book gives great honor to physicians and pharmacists and considers their skills God-ordained and blessed. Their people are instructed in verse 9-12 to "pray to the Lord, and he will heal you," "give up your faults," "cleanse your heart from sin," and offer a "sweet-smelling sacrifice" prior to consulting their physician. These words of wisdom encourage and embrace seeking a doctor for health issues.

The remaining chapters in this book discuss the Jewish grieving process, the educated business person, the wisdom of the scribes, wickedness, and a few other social issues. From chapter 44 to 50 a tribute to honored Jewish ancestors is given from Enoch to Simon, Son of Onias. They are interesting chapters—not to be forgotten. The final chapter concludes with a prayer from Jesus son of Sirach.

This book provides the reader with a variety of advice. It is not hard to understand why Sirach used this book as part of his curriculum in teaching scholars. It is a book of advice that children as well as adults can use. However, within all the contents of this text and the text that was not included in my writings, the same reoccurring message is evident—"Keep the Faith."

Book of
Baruch

Introduction and Summary

According to NRSV commentary, Baruch was a friend of Jeremiah who was also taken from Jerusalem to Egypt with Jeremiah. Baruch and Jeremiah both died in Egypt. This book gives us information about Jeremiah after captivity that does not exist in the Old Testament book of Jeremiah.

The book is a letter written to the people and priests of Jerusalem after it was destroyed. The purpose of this book is to comfort the people and lead them to repentance. Remember, the people are trying to rationalize why all of theses terrible things have happened to them and why God allowed their temple to be destroyed.

Throughout this book, the prophet is encouraging the people to turn from their evil ways so that God would bless them again. The poetic beauty of their renewal of hope is described in Chapter 5: 1-4 as follows:

> "Take off the garment of your sorrow and affliction, O Jerusalem, and put on forever the beauty of the glory from God. Put on the robe of the righteousness that comes from God; put on your head the diadem of the glory of the Everlasting; for God will show your splendor everywhere under heaven. For God will give you evermore the name, "Righteous Peace, Godly Glory."" (NRSV)[15]

This book encourages the people to have faith in God and to persevere in trials and tribulations—God will deliver them.

---

[15] *The Harper Collins Study Bible: New Revised Standard Version.* Society of Biblical Literature. Harper San Francisco. Fulham Palace Road, London W6 8JB. 1989

Book of
the Letter of
Jeremiah

Book of the Letter of Jeremiah

Introduction and Summary

In this book, the writer is trying to educate the people about other gods, lead them to repentance and worship of the true and only God. It is prophesied to the people that they will linger in exile for many years because of their sins—up to seven generations. They are warned to refrain from worshiping the idols of Babylon. It is believed to have been written between the fourth and second century B.C.E.

Jeremiah was the prophet that nobody wanted to listen to before exile. He was deported around 597 B.C.E. During this time of exile, Judaism was in contact with the religions of Egypt, Syria, Mesopotamia, and Greece. These religions used statues for gods in their religious ceremonies. There was a strong movement among Israel to make their God the only deity in the area, so they protested the image of other god's and their enemies retaliated.

A portion of text found in this book is also mentioned by the writer of 2 Maccabees 2:1-3. This book took on the title of Jeremiah because it supports the scriptures found in the Old Testament. A small portion of this scripture (verses 43-44) was discovered at Cave #7 at Qumran[16].

The book encourages the people to remain faithful to God and endure the trials and tribulations they will encounter.

---

[16]   *The Harper Collins Study Bible: New Revised Standard Version.* Society of Biblical Literature. Harper San Francisco. Fulham Palace Road, London W6 8JB. 1989

The Prayer of
Azariah and the Song
of the Three Jews

The Prayer of Azariah and
the Song of the Three Jews

Introduction and Summary

Greek and Latin versions of the book of Daniel contain scriptures that are not in the Jewish or Protestant canons and referred to the above title[17]. It is believed these additions were inserted between the second and first century B.C.E. and at the time Latin was becoming the common language.

It contains the prayers and praises of those who were in the furnace with Daniel. It details the events that have taken place within Israel and describes Israel's oppression under their new rulers The prayers of the three men in the furnace is a testimony and message of hope and faith to the persecuted.

The book encourages the people to remain faithful to God and endure the trials and tribulations they will encounter just as Daniel and his friends did while they were imprisoned in the furnace.

---

[17] *The Harper Collins Study Bible: New Revised Standard Version*. Society of Biblical Literature. Harper San Francisco. Fulham Palace Road, London W6 8JB. 1989

91

Book of
Susanna

Introduction

The story of Susanna is a story about two men of leadership with a passion for self-gratification. Their personal desires cause them to assault Susanna's credibility and reputation. This same passion for self-gratification runs rampant in America today.

In order to understand this story, we must understand that rape is not always forced upon someone physically, but can also be forced upon someone through social threats. Either way, it is an attack on a woman's reputation and creditability. Although the men in this story had enough self-discipline to prevent them from physically forcing themselves on Susanna, they still attacked her credibility and reputation by offering unfavorable choices.

Americans tend to act like they understand the problem of rape, but in reality many do not. According to RAINN's website, every 2 minutes an American citizen is being raped. Sixty percent of rapes are not reported to law enforcement, and 75% of the victims know their rapist. In addition, 15 of 16 rapists will not do the time for the crime[18]. These statistics vary from report to report and are compiled among many different ages. No matter what report you look at, the evidence is there, many rapes are not reported and leave women suffering silently because friends and family members do not step up and get involved in promoting justice just as Susanna's family and friends advocated for her.

---

[18] *Statistics.* RAINN Rape Abuse & Incest National Network. 2009. *www.rainn.org/statistics*

Summary

Although the religious leaders' passion for self-gratification does not motivate them to force themselves upon the woman, they use their leadership positions to unfairly attack her credibility and self-respect. Since Susanna refuses to submit to their request for sex, they publicly accuse her of having intercourse with a young man who is not her husband and almost have her executed. She puts her faith in God, and is delivered.

The story begins with two elders of her household that are obsessed by the beauty of Susanna, a wealthy married woman. On one hot day, they make plans to hide in her garden and wait for her to bathe. After she sends her maids out to retrieve her olive oil and ointments, the elders get up and approach her. They tell her how they are burning with passion to sleep with her and if she does not consent to have sex with them, they will tell everybody she was with another man. She realizes that both options are unfavorable and decides to refuse their demands and screams for help. Her screams get the attention of the servants, and the elders quickly tell the servants that she has had sex with another man. Since the elders are highly respected in society, the servants believe them and are ashamed of Susanna. The case goes to court, and the elders proceed to tell the lie that Susanna had slept with another man. The people and the judges believe these men of authority and condemn her to death. Susanna prays to God, and the Lord sends a man named Daniel.

Now it is noted by many Bible scholars that the name Daniel may be a pun. The name Daniel means "God is my judge" and that is exactly what this man did.

Daniel discerns that Susanna's accusers have falsely stated that she had intercourse with another man. He commands the elders to be cross-examined in separate areas and the elders are caught in their lie. He calls them false prophets and references the story about the two false prophets found in Jeremiah 29:20-23. He informs the people to not make hasty decisions and to check out their stories before they condemn someone and engage in gossip. Then the sentence that was given to Susanna was revoked and given to the two elders (Deut 19:18-21) and they were put to death.

In this story, it is not just Susanna's credibility that is at stake, but also the credibility and safety of her family and friends that defend her and refuse to support the false accusations of authority. Her friends and family will not unjustly endure the shame the elders try to make her and her family bear.

This is not only a message to have faith in God and seek him for deliverance, but it is also a message to all people to take a brave stand against such injustice. Over the past many years, molestation and rape has been committed by America's religious leaders, (Protestant and Catholic alike) as well as other leaders within America's communities. It has been found that many people were aware of the crimes, but refused to report it. People were more worried about tarnishing the leader's reputation than assisting the innocent victim and maintaining their good reputation.

This book teaches us five things. First, it encourages God's people to remain faithful despite an attack on their respect and credibility. Secondly, God's people are reminded that he is the judge and the Bible teaches us that all things will eventually come before God for final judgment. Thirdly, it reminds us that corruption can exist among religious authorities; fourthly, it encourages families to strongly support each other; and lastly, it reminds us to abstain from gossip that can be started by either/and men, women, and/or leaders.

Book of Bel
And
the Dragon

Introduction and Summary

The NRSV commentary explains that this book describes another part of Daniel's life and experience in the lion's den located in ancient Near East that is not found in the Old Testament.[19] The book was written between the 3rd and 1st century B.C.E and describes how Daniel refuses to worship a clay idol of Babylon called Bel. He tells the king that their idol is not alive and the king tells him he is wrong. The king tells him he can prove it because the idol eats the food that is brought to him everyday. Daniel knows that there is a hidden door under the idol and the food is consumed by the priests and their wives and children; not the idol. However the king is either naive or refuses to tell the truth about the disappearing food, so Daniel places ashes on the floor by the hidden door under the idol, and the doors to the room are sealed that evening with the king's signet.

That night, the priest, wives, and children come into the room through the hidden door and consume the food. The next morning, the king and Daniel enter the room. The king notes that the seal is still on the doors and praises Bel when he enters the room and finds the food completely consumed. Daniel then points out the footprints of the priests, wives, and children in the ashes on the floor. The king becomes angry and has the priests, wives, and children put to death. He gives Bel to Daniel to do as he wishes. Daniel destroys the idol and its temple.

---

[19]   *The Harper Collins Study Bible: New Revised Standard Version.* Society of Biblical Literature. Harper San Francisco. Fulham Palace Road, London W6 8JB. 1989

Then the king proceeds to show Daniel the great Dragon that the Babylonians worship. He tells Daniel this was a living god that he needs to worship. Daniel refuses to worship the Dragon stating he only worships the Lord his God. He tells the king he will kill the dragon without a sword or club. The king grants Daniel permission to try to kill the Dragon.

Daniel boils up some pitch, fat, and hair and makes them into cakes. He feeds them to the Dragon. The Dragon bursts open and dies. The Babylonians are angry. They accuse the king of becoming a Jew. They tell the king if he does not hand Daniel over to them, they will kill him and his household. The king hands Daniel over to the people and they put him in the lions' den.

On the seventh day, to the king's surprise, Daniel survives and is not eaten by the lions. The king praises Daniel's God, removes Daniel from the lions' den, and throws in the people who sought to kill him. They are killed immediately by the lions.

The book encourages the people to remain faithful to God, to refrain from worshipping other gods, and to stand strong and endure any trials and tribulations they may face.

Book of I
Maccabees

Introduction

Fiction or non-fiction—that is the question. This book is about a family with the last name of Maccabees and their line of priesthood during the turbulent times of revolving powers after the death of Alexander the Great. Some historical facts can be confirmed by historical documents while others are questioned. It is also a story about wars after wars after wars. If you like war stories, this one will interest you. You might get a copy of the Apocrypha so that you can dig deeper into the historical contents of this story.

The Maccabee name is also described as a movement. An interesting fact that I found in the commentary section of The Harper Collins Bible suggests that the communities in charge of the Dead Sea Scrolls (found at Qumran) may have been early followers of the Maccabean movement and withdrew when the Maccabees gained the high priesthood and the temple worship[20].

---

[20] *The Harper Collins Study Bible: New Revised Standard Version.* Society of Biblical Literature. Harper San Francisco. Fulham Palace Road, London W6 8JB. 1989. (page 1647)

Summary

The book begins after the death of Alexander the Great who had divided his kingdom among his most "honored officers" that he had known since he was a young boy. Upon the reign of these men, great wickedness spread through the land.

A group of Jewish rebels began to join forces with a ruler known as Antiochus Epiphanes. He was the son of King Antiochus and the first ruler in the 137th years of the Kingdom of the Greeks. The Jewish rebels erected a gymnasium in Jerusalem according to Gentile tradition. In addition they removed the mark of circumcision and forsook their Holy Covenant.

Wars began as King Antiochus captured and robbed Egypt. King Antiochus invaded Israel and robbed their temple with much bloodshed and war. Then he sent his people to take over the City of David and the temple. He informed the Jewish people that they must adopt his religion and threatened them with death if they did not conform and submit to his request.

A Jewish man named Mattathias and his sons refused to worship as King Antiochus commanded, and Mattathias killed a Jewish rebel who was loyal and obedient to the king's orders as well as one of the king's officers. After this event, Mattathias and his sons went into hiding. After the king massacred a group of Jews taking refuge in the wilderness, Mattathias and his sons began to organize troops to fight against the king.

At the time Mattathias was near death, he assigned Simon as their father and Judas Maccabees as a commander of their troops. Judas became a well-known valiant and successful leader. The Jews won many battles under the command of Judas who looked to God to deliver them as they fought. Although they fought with few men and inferior weapons, they still won many battles and attributed their deliverance to God.

After defeating the Lysias army, they captured their sanctuary only to find it profaned. The gates had been burnt. They began to restore the sanctuary and the Gentiles became angry and declared they would destroy the Jews. However, they did not.

Judas continued to be victorious in many battles. King Antiochus was upset over Judas' victories. Soon after, King Antiochus was stricken with illness, he gave his kingdom to Philip and then died. The food supply in the kingdom decreased and the people pleaded with Philip to agree to live in peace with the Jews. Although Philip sent an offer of peace to the Jews, the king changed his mind once he set his eyes on the Jews' mighty fortress. Again, more fighting and killings occurred. Nicanor, an honored prince of the king, was sent to destroy the Jews. He made plans to kidnap Judas and his attempt failed. The Jewish priests prayed for vengeance against Nicanor, and he was killed the next day while in battle.

In the meantime, the Roman armies and government grew in numbers and strength, so Judas sought an alliance with Rome. He communicated his terms of agreement to them. Shortly afterwards, Judas died in battle against the army of Bacchides. Jonathan and Simon buried Judas and all of Israel mourned over his death for many days.

Jonathan is assigned Judas' position and the Jewish rebels were ever present in many places throughout Israel. A great famine occurred and Bacchides sought revenge against Judah by searching for his friends to make "sport" of them. It is written that the Jews felt more distressed on that day than on the day the prophets no longer appeared among them.

Once again, the wars began to cease. Jonathan stayed in Michmash and assumed the position of Judge. He removed the ungodly from the land and rebuilt and restored the city of Jerusalem. King Alexander sought peace with Jonathan and appointed Jonathan high priest of his nation. Jonathan accepted the appointment.

King Demetrius became jealous and sought to seek peace with Jonathan by exempting the Jews from payments of tributes, salt tax, and crown levies among other things. Jonathan did not accept King Demetrius' promises because of his past problems in dealing with him. King Alexander and Demetrius go to war with each other and King Demetrius is killed. Although King Alexander gained control of his nation, Demetrius' son soon came to power and challenged Jonathan and his troops.

The king of Egypt tried to gain control of Alexander's kingdom. Then, peace resumed under the leadership of young King Demetrius until he reneged on his promises to Jonathan and war broke out again. In the midst of a moment of promised peace, Jonathon and some of his men are betrayed and captured. All of Israel mourned for those that had been killed and planned to battle again. Simon became their new commander. Trypho killed Jonathan and Israel mourned.

So the young King Demetrius sought peace with Simon and was captured by Trypho. Later, another period of peace began. Simon is elected high priest of the Jews as the Jews gained their independence and respect among nations. As time goes on, a much older Simon finds Judah under oppression once again. Simon assigned his sons, Judas and John to take his brother's and his role. Sadly, Judas and two of his sons, Mattathias and Judas are killed by Ptolemy and his men. John survived and becomes the new leader and high priest.

Among all the wars, bloodshed, and power shifts, the message within this book encourages believers to remain faithful during trials and tribulations.

Book of
II Maccabees

Book of II Maccabees

Introduction

Many of the events in this story are true. This book provides events leading up to "subsequent exploits" of Judea up to 161 B.C.E[21] It describes the political corruptive behaviors of the Jewish high-priesthood and how Judas Maccabees fought for justice. As the "ideal Jewish warrior," Judas Maccabees prays prior to the battles. After the battles are fought, he takes time to thank God. He religiously follows the commandments to keep the Sabbath Day holy. This book is not a continuation of I Maccabees, but provides in-depth details of the life of the first warrior, Judas Maccabees. The first Maccabees warrior's life begins in chapter 3 of I Maccabees.

Historical facts of the writing of this book are found in Chapter 2:19-32. The chapter describes how it was condensed from a five volume work to a single book and the difficulties, concerns, and considerations that needed to be made in order to keep the content pure.

Chapter 2:23 indicates that Jason of Cycrene wrote the book. According to the NRSV commentary, the current writing that was condensed may not closely match the original five volume text since we do not have Jason's original writings. Jason's five volume book and the condensed version were both written in Greek. According to the NRSV commentary, the Greek is not "as biblical as I Maccabees." It

---

[21] *The Harper Collins Study Bible: New Revised Standard Version.* Society of Biblical Literature. Harper San Francisco. Fulham Palace Road, London W6 8JB. 1989

is believed that Jason wrote this book soon after these things occurred. The account ends before Judas' death. It is believed that the condensed text was completed by 124 B.C.E. which is the date on the "cover letter" which is recorded in II Maccabees 1: 1-9.

Book of II Maccabees

Summary

The chapter begins with the celebration of booths. The priest's prayer in offering of sacrifice indicates they continue to look for a deliverer and victory over the Gentile nations. (verse 24-29) During the sacrifice, Nehemiah uses fire in a very unordinary way that draws much attention to him. The king is so amazed with Nehemiah's use of fire that he labels it to be holy.

In chapter 2, prophet Jeremiah instructs the Jews while they were being exiled to take some of the fire with them and also ordered them to remain faithful to God and not forsake any of God's commandments. During exile, Nehemiah collects all of the books about kings, all the written documents of King David, and the communications of kings regarding "votive offerings". Judas also collects writings that have disappeared during the battles. After all books are collected, they inform the Jewish people to contact them if they wish to obtain them for their own use in the future.

Beginning in verse 19, the writer summarizes the victories of Judas Maccabees and his brothers among their enemies and the purification of the temple. The text continues to describe how Jason of Cyrene carefully takes on the responsibility of completing the difficult task of compiling five books into one book entitled 2 Maccabees.

The story begins in chapter 3. The writer describes how some of the money deposited in the temple treasury specifically for the orphans, widows, and Hyrcanus, the son of a man named Tobias amounted to a

sum of four hundred talents of silver and two hundred of gold. A man
named Simon incorrectly reported this amount.

Heliodorus, a man who was commanded from the king, stated this
money was to be seized for the king's treasury. At this point, the writer
begins to detail how the priests bowed down before the alter and

> " . . . called toward heaven upon him who had given the law
> about deposits, that he should keep them safe for those who
> had deposited them. (verse 15)

It appears the priests are calling upon God to help them in maintaining
the laws of keeping the deposits as God has commanded them since,
at this point, the priests do not appear to be corrupt in exercising their
priestly obligations and responsibilities. Not only do the priests look
towards God, but people and some women wearing sackcloth run out
into the streets and come together with their hands outreached towards
heaven in prayer realizing their laws and commandments from God
were about to be violated. The people are calling to "the Lord."

"The power of God" appeared and Heliodorus is attacked by the
front hoofs of a horse. Its rider is armed with weapons of gold and
accompanied by two young men who flogged Heliodorus. Although
Heliodorus was carried away on a stretcher, he is healed.

The young warriors request him to be appreciative of their high
priest, Onias, who has prayed for him. The Jews credit God's power for
this victory. It is clear that in this same chapter, God (verse 28) and Lord
are of the same identity.

In chapter 4, a high priest named Onias is verbally attacked by a
man named Simon. Onias observes Simon becoming full of hate and
rivalry. Simon's negative behaviors intensify more as they become
fueled by Appollonius son of Menestheus and governor of Coelesyria

and Phoenicia resulting in murders. This prompts Onias to go to the king to secure a nonviolent agreement and to end Simon's recklessness.

After the death of Seleucus, Antiochus (also known as Epiphanes) reigned. Onias' brother, Jason, secures the high priesthood through "corruption" by promising the king money, a gymnasium, and young people to use it. Once Jason is in office, he evasively changes his fellow citizens to the Greek style of living. The Jewish priests begin to neglect their duties and follow and honor the unlawful practices of the Greeks. (Remember, the people are warned of securing friendships with enemies in the Wisdom of Jesus Son of Sirach in Chapter 13.)

After three years, Jason sends the brother of Simon, Menelaus, to carry money to the king. When he meets the king, he exalts him and obtains the kings favor by offering him a higher offer for the priesthood than Jason. The king assigns Menelaus the high priesthood position. Menelaus fails to make the proposed payments to the king as he promised.

During this period, the temple vessels are given away and Onias is unjustly murdered by Andronicus at the request of Menelaus. The Jews and other nations (including the Greeks) greatly grieve over the death of Onias. King Antiochus is also grieved and Andronicus is punished.

Next, the Jews are under attack by a man named Lysimachus. Menelaus is the instigator of such attacks. He provides a kickback to spare himself from being punished. He is not removed from office because of the greedy behavior of higher authority. His evilness continues to intensify. The young, old males, women, and children are destroyed. Young females and babies are massacred.

In chapter 5, a great number of Jews are killed under the pretense of peace as described in verse 26. However, Judas Maccabees manages to escape the massacre. As the wars continue, we find in chapter 6 that the

Jews are asked to no longer honor the laws of their ancestors. Verses 3-6 describe how the Jewish temples are used by the Greeks and follows:

> "Harsh and utterly grievous was the onslaught of evil. For the temple was filled with debauchery and reveling by the Gentiles, who dallied with prostitutes and had intercourse with women within the sacred precincts, and besides brought in things for sacrifice that were unfit. The altar was covered with abominable offerings that were forbidden by the laws. People could neither keep the Sabbath, nor observe the festivals of their ancestors, not so much as confess themselves to be Jews."

The details of the battles are gruesome. The people believed that all of these horrid experiences were the result of their past sins and this was God's way of punishing them. The author must have felt that he needed to explain this situation to future readers and added the following text found in chapter 6: 12-17:

> "Now I urge those who read this book not to be depressed by such calamities, but to recognize that these punishments were designed not to destroy but to discipline our people. In fact, it is a sign of great kindness not to let the impious alone for long, but to punish them immediately. For in the case of the other nations the Lord waits patiently to punish them until they have reached the full measure of their sins; but he does not deal in this way with us, in order that he may not take vengeance on us afterward when our sins have reached their height. Therefore he never withdraws his mercy from us. Although he disciplines us with calamities, he does not forsake his own

people. Let what we have said serve as a reminder; we must go on briefly with the story."

At the end of Chapter 6, the writer writes of the Jews who have died the death of martyrs. This type of death is not found among the life of Abraham, David, Moses, or any of the other great faithful men of the Bible. However, this sort of faith is the beginning of those things to come and described in the NT. These deaths are described as follows:

"When he was about to die under the blows, he groaned aloud and said: "It is clear to the Lord in his holy knowledge that, though I might have been saved from death, I am enduring terrible sufferings in my body under this bearing, but in my soul I am glad to suffer these things because I fear him.""" (6:30-31)

"The king fell into a rage, and gave orders to have pans and caldrons heated. These were heated immediately, and he commanded that the tongue of their spokesman be cut out and that they scalp him and cut off his hands and feet, while the rest of the brothers and the mother looked on. When he was utterly helpless, the king ordered them to take him to the fire, still breathing, and to fry him in a pan. The smoke from the pan spread widely, but the brothers and their mother encouraged one another to die nobly saying. "The Lord God is watching over us and in truth has compassion on us, as Moses declared in his song that bore witness against the people to their faces, when he said, "And he will have compassion on his servants." (7:3-6)

"After him, the third was the victim of the sport. When it was demanded, he quickly put out his tongue and courageously stretched forth his hands, and said nobly, I got these from Heaven, and because of his laws I disdain them, and from him I hope to get them back again." As a result the king himself and those with him were astonished at the young man's spirit, for he regarded his sufferings as nothing. After he too had died, they maltreated and tortured the fourth in the same way." (7:10-13)

"When he was near death, he said, "One cannot but choose to die at the hands of mortals and to cherish the hope God gives of being raised again by him. But for you there will be no resurrection to life!" (7:14)

"Next they brought forward the fifth and maltreated him. But he looked at the king, and said, "Because you have authority among mortals, though you also are mortal, you do what you please, But do not think that God has forsaken our people. Keep on, and see how his mighty power will torture you and your descendants!"" (7:15-17)

""I beg you, my child, to look at the heaven and the earth and see everything that is in them, and recognize that God did not make them out of things that existed. And in the same way the human race came into being. Do not fear this butcher, but prove worthy of your brothers. Accept death so that in God's mercy I may get you back again along with your brothers" . . . The king fell into a rage, and handled him worse than the others, being exasperated at his scorn. So he died in

his integrity, putting his whole trust in the Lord. Last of all,
the mother died after her sons." (7:28-29 and 39-41)

Here are the words Jesus said to those who died while standing up for
righteousness:

""'Blessed are those who are persecuted for righteousness'
sake, for theirs is the kingdom of heaven. Blessed are you
when people revile you and persecute you and utter all kinds
of evil against you falsely on my account. Rejoice and be glad,
for your reward is great in heaven, for in the same way they
persecuted the prophets who were before you.'"" (Matthew
5:10-11)

Judas Maccabees revolts in Chapter 8:3 and the spoils of the battles
are given to the orphans, widows, and those that had been tortured as
described in chapter 8:28 and 30.

While traveling to strike against the Jews, Antichus becomes ill. His
illness causes him to die a slow and gruesome death. He decides to pray
to God and hopes for complete healing of this disease. He pledges to God
that he will free all Jews and promises equality with the citizens of Athens.
In addition, he promises to return the vessels to the sanctuary and vows to
become a Jew. As he believes he is nearing his death (v18), he composes a
letter to the Jews. This letter is found at the end of chapter 9. In this letter,
he describes his illness to the Jews and announces his son as the successor
of his throne. He explains to the Jews that "in hope" he believes he will
recover from this illness He promises them that they will be treated with
the same amount of kindness and policy by his son. He dies.

Maccabees purifies the temple and asks God to discipline them
(10:4) with "forbearance" and prays that God would not allow an

unholy nation to rule over them in the future. Many battles are fought to establish and maintain their freedom. In these battles, the writer states they are aided by heavenly forces (10:29-30 and in 11:6-8). In Chapter 11, the heavenly force is described as dressed in white and handling weapons of gold.

King Antiochus' letter to Lysias is found in chapter 11:22-26 and very interesting. Following this letter, the people of Joppa deceive the Jews into believing they are their friends, but take them out to sea and throw them overboard. When King Judas hears of the news, he gives orders to assault the men, burn their boats and harbor and murder those who had gone there for safety. He also attacks the Jamnites who are making the same plans as the people in Joppa did. They are destroyed by God (Chapter 12). In one battle, the Jews slaughtered so many, the lake appears as blood

In 2 Maccabees 12:32, we find another reference made to the celebration of Pentecost. Again, the only time we find this Jewish tradition labeled as Pentecost is in the Apocrypha and subtly hinted in the New Testament.

Monetary atonement is made for the sins of those Jews who died in battle and were found with the sacred token from the Jamnia's idols under their tunic. (12:40). Nicanor's death is described in chapter 15: 28, 36, 37 and 38 as follows:

> "When the action was over and they were returning with joy, the recognized Nicanor, lying dead, in full armor . . . And they all decreed by public vote never to let this day go underserved, but to celebrate the thirteenth day of the twelfth month—which is called Adar in the Aramaic language—the day before Mordecai's day. This then, is how matters turned

out with Nicanor, and from that time the city has been in the possession of the Hebrews. So I will here end my story."

The writer concludes his story as follows:

"If it is well told and to the point, that is what I myself desired; if it is poorly done and mediocre, that was the best I could do. For just as it is harmful to drink wine alone, or, again, to drink water alone, while wine mixed with water is sweet and delicious and enhances one's enjoyment, so also the style of the story delights the ears of those who read the work. And here will be the end." (15:38-39)

Through all of the wars, deaths, and oppression; Jesus Christ was still born through the blood of King David as prophesied.

Conclusion

Conclusion

In the first section of the Apocrypha, we find stories of people enduring difficult times under their leadership. In faith, they are delivered from their oppressive situations and some become admired heroes. However, as we head towards the books of wisdom, we find social theories that suggest that deliverance may not come so easily during this life time.

As we move past the books of wisdom, we also learn that religious authorities have the potential to be unreliable and fail the people miserably, and innocent Israelites are killed for their beliefs in God. However, despite opposition, Israel is determined to rebuild her temple, nation, and faith. One consistent message throughout the books of the Apocrypha is to "keep the faith" despite oppressive trials, and tribulations.

My book is not a commentary, but a simple review from my perspective. It is my intent to encourage other people to read, study, and research the Apocrypha in order to have a better understanding of the culture of that time before-and during the life of Christ. Knowing and understanding history, for that matter, is important to me.

The Apocrypha acts as a binding agent between the New and Old Testament to encourage us to trust in God through fiction and non-fiction stories. In this life, although we may be up against powers and principalities of greed, control, and self-gratification; we can also embrace the message of hope found within these books knowing that our God is our ultimate deliverer. True social justice will let "judgment roll down as waters and righteousness as a mighty stream." (Amos 5:24 KJV)

Glossary

(Defining words used in this book)

Apocrypha—A group of books and parts of books that are included in the Roman Catholic and Orthodox Bibles. These books are uncommonly found in the Protestant Bibles. If they are included, they are separated into a section titled "Apocrypha". These books were rejected by most Protestant's during the Reformation.

Calvinism's Westminster Confession—It is the reformed confession of faith among the Calvinist theological tradition developed in 1646 by Westminster Assembly. It became and still is the 'subordinate standard' of doctrine in the Church of Scotland and among Presbyterian churches worldwide.

Canon—The books in the Bible that are accepted as being the "inspired word".

Babylonian Deportation or **Exile**—The act of removing the Jews from their homeland and into captivity in Babylon (587-538 B.C.E.)

Geneva Bible—This Bible is known as the Bible of the 16th century Protestant reformation that was translated into English.

Judiasm—The practice of Jewish religion.

Qumran Cave—This location is not mentioned in the Bible. However, it is a historical site of a community close to an area where the Dead Sea Scrolls were found in early 1947.

Sackcloth—A rough material made out of goat's or camel's hair. It was worn when an individual was in distress or mourning.

Septuagint—A book compiled of Hebrew scriptures written in Greek.

Torah—This term is used by the Jews to reference their Jewish legal traditions, Law, and their first five books of the Bible.

Vulgate—The Latin version of the Bible written by Jerome (ca. 347-420) as requested by Pope Damasus.

Bibliography

Eerdmans Dictionary of the Bible. Wm B. Eerdmans Publishing Co. Grand Rapids, MI 49503. 2000

Statistics. RAINN Rape, Abuse & Incest National Network. 2009. www.rainn.org/statistics

The Harper Collins Study Bible: New Revised Standard Version. Society of Biblical Literature. Harper San Francisco. Fulham Palace Road, London W6 8JB. 1989

The New Interpreter's Study Bible: New Revised Standard Version with the Apocrypha. Abingdon Press. Nashville, TN 1989

CPSIA information can be obtained at www.ICGtesting.com
Printed in the USA
LVOW13s0358081113

360279LV00002B/168/P